SALFORD
Reds
RUGBY LEAGUE
Sheffield Eagles
LONDON RUGBY LEAGUE
SUPER LEAGUE
BRADFORD BULLS
PSG
RUGBY LEAGUE
LONDON
RLFC
£5.50
UK ONLY

Contents

Below: ***Bobby Goulding of St. Helens in full flight***

Written by John Robinson
Pictures © Varley Wilkinson, Leeds, except 12/13 © BSKYB LTD
Designed by Perry Tate Design
Edited by John Malam

Main cover photo: Andy Farrell of Wigan Warriors and Great Britain

Published in Great Britain by
World International Ltd.,
Deanway Technology Centre,
Wilmslow Road,
Handforth, Cheshire SK9 3FB.
Printed in Italy.
ISBN 0-7498-3389-0

Statistics and information contained in this publication are correct to 1 June 1997

Go Forward! with Andy Farrell

These are exciting times for Super League as we herald a new era for the game, and I am looking forward to every minute. So much has changed for the better in such a short time. Summer rugby is here to stay, and there are exciting new challenges around every corner.

Sometimes I feel like one of the characters in the television series Star Trek – boldly going where no one has gone before! The quality of rugby served up in Super League has been breathtaking. New standards have been set for fitness and stamina.

It was also an inspired idea to introduce a global event so that our clubs could take on the best sides from Australia and New Zealand on a regular basis. It fired the imagination of fans who wanted something different – and there is no better way of measuring our progress in Europe.

We have always believed that Rugby League is the best game in the world. Now we have the chance to prove it with vision and adventure. The demands on players have never been greater, but then so are the rewards.

As we build for the new millennium, it is gratifying that so many young players are looking to Rugby League for a full-time career. Hopefully, I have set an example – and will continue to do so. It's a great life, believe me!

A Farrell

Andy Farrell

BOLD VENTURE

Bomb Squad

Bobbie Goulding is the head of 'Bomber Command' at St. Helens after mastering the tactical high kick which causes panic in defence lines and often produces tries.

Skipper Goulding, a cunning half-back with a strong will to win, practices the kick for hour upon hour at training. And no one does it better anywhere in the world. The idea is to kick the ball high in the air – usually on the fourth or fifth tackle – as an attacking strategy deep inside the opposition's half. If the kick is well executed, the ball will hang in the air long enough for attacking players to move forward and gain favourable positions to regain possession. As the ball drops like a bomb from the sky, it is often the defending full-back who has the unenviable task of fielding the kick close to his own try line.

Goulding has perfected the technique of sending the ball soaring up to 100 feet into the air. By the time it comes down, the unhappy receiver is usually surrounded by eager Saints players ready to pounce on any mistake.The tactic puts tremendous pressure on the defence, especially when the ball-taker finds himself caught in open space unsupported by team-mates.

Not surprisingly, the 'bomb' is a favourite weapon in Goulding's extensive bag of tricks. The kick was known as an 'up and under' before being re-named following a trend in Australia. Yet even the Aussies, who became such great exponents that it became almost an art form, would have nothing to teach 25-year-old Goulding.

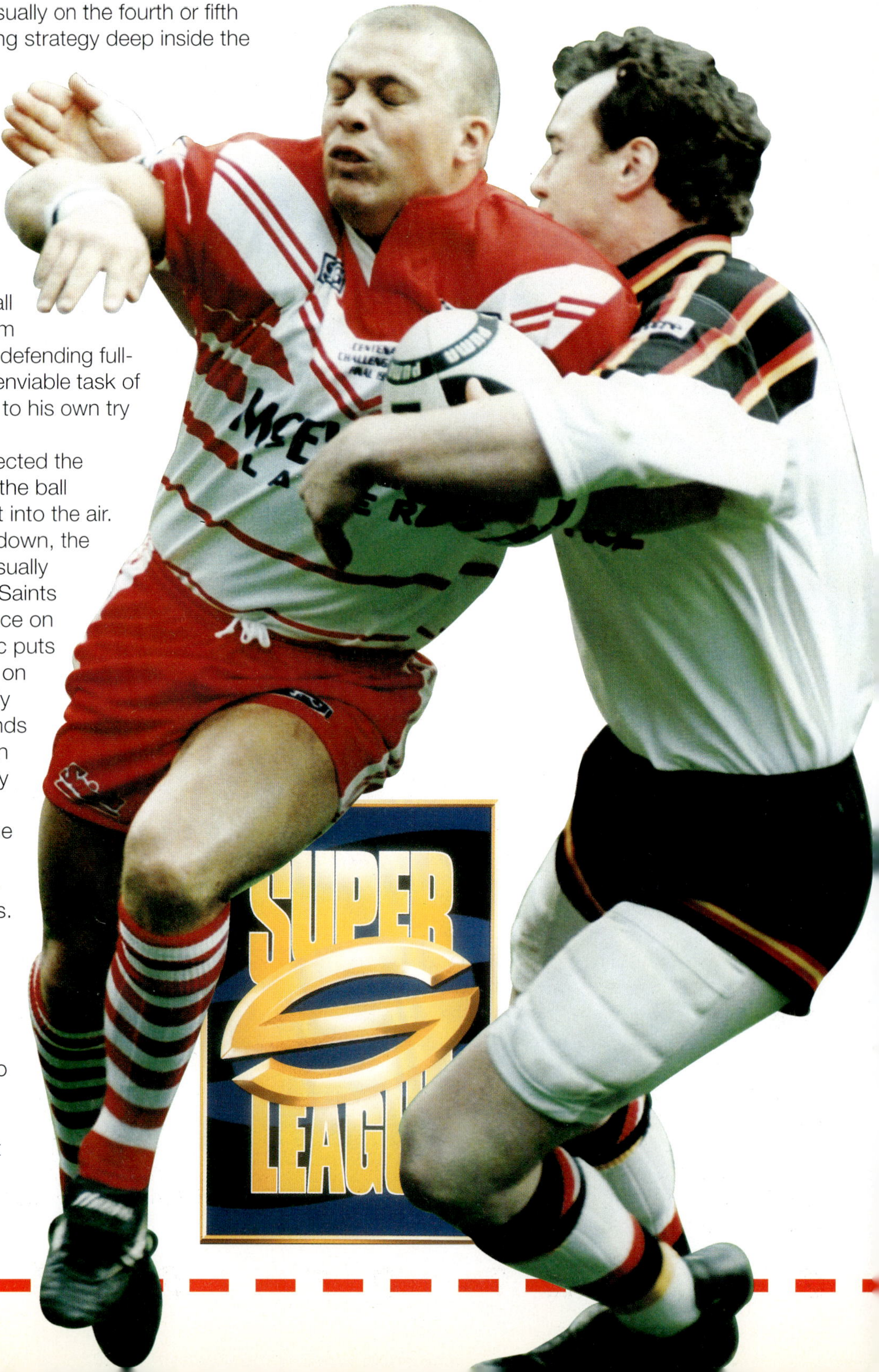

Coming through! Bobbie attempts to slip out of a tackle

"With the 'bomb', the height of the kick is not as important as where the ball comes down. I generally want it to travel no further forward than 35 yards."

Left: ***Whack! Bobbie launches a high kick***
Above: ***Bobbie's in charge as Saints go on the attack***

FACTFILE

Full Name: Bobbie Goulding
Date of Birth: 4 February 1972
Birthplace: Widnes
Height: 5ft 7in
Weight: 13st
Club: St. Helens
Position: Scrum half
Previous Clubs: Wigan, Leeds, Widnes
Caps: Great Britain 14, England 5, Under-21s 5
Medals: Championship 1990, 1991 (Wigan), Challenge Cup 1990, 1991 (Wigan), 1996 (St. Helens); Super League Championship 1996
Tours: Papua New Guinea and New Zealand 1990; Papua New Guinea, Fiji and New Zealand 1996
Honours: Young Player of the Year 1990; First Division Player of the Year 1995

Another Goulding speciality is the shallow cross-field kick aimed at bouncing in the corner at just the right spot for his wingers to re-gather and score. But Goulding is quick to point out that any kick is only as good as the chase which follows it. He says: "We have had tremendous success with the 'bomb' at St. Helens because players such as Steve Prescott and Tommy Martyn are so quick off the mark to put pressure on the opposition. They are like greyhounds out of the trap, whether the kick is high or just a routine chip ahead. I call the play so that they know what sort of kick is coming up.

"With the 'bomb', the height of the kick is not as important as where the ball comes down. I generally want it to travel no further forward than 35 yards.

"It is difficult to defend against a well-executed 'bomb'. No one has devised an effective counter-plan. I can understand defending full-backs having nightmares. I would hate to be in their shoes in these situations! Technically, the high-kick is not difficult. But it is important to make a good contact under the ball and drive the kicking foot upwards. It also helps if the body leans backwards."

A prime example of Goulding's deadly aerial power came in the Silk Cut Challenge Cup Final of 1996. With Bradford Bulls dominant and leading by fourteen points, Goulding unleashed a series of towering 'bombs'. Three tries later the game was won and Saints lifted the Cup for the first time in 20 years.

Kris Radlinski

Wigan's Central Park is a home from home for Kris the 21-year-old Warrior. He is constantly at the ground working on his game. Here is a typical day in his life.

8.30am

A bowl of Shredded Wheat and a cup of tea puts me in fine fettle and I watch breakfast TV for a while. On match days I often lie-in and spend an extra couple of hours sleeping. Then my mum will sometimes treat me to breakfast in bed and serve up tea, toast and jam. My bedroom is just the way I like it. It's full of baseball caps which I collect as a hobby.

9.30am

The Treatment Room at Wigan's Central Park opens for business so that the physios can look at anyone suffering from injuries or bumps and bruises. We receive first class attention. I go along even when I am feeling OK, just to have a rub down and a chat with the rest of the lads.

Then I head for the gym for a session on the weights, which is a regular feature of our training to develop upper-body strength. The team also has a number of training sessions every week when we concentrate on ball skills and fitness drills. These can be organised at any time. I have always enjoyed training.

There is a professional atmosphere at the club. Preparation for matches is extremely thorough and competition for places is keen. But it is not always serious stuff. Sometimes we have a knock-about wrestling contest. Take on Terry O'Connor and it's like being hit by a truck!

12.30pm

Lunch is often served for the players at the club after a morning training session. But on other occasions a group of us will relax by taking a stroll around town and calling in at a local café for a quick bite to eat.

The other players call me 'Rad' or 'Radders', and I am often stopped in the street to sign autographs. Lots of people want to know the origin of the Radlinski surname. The fact is I am Wigan-born of

Kris shows the skills which have taken him to the top with Wigan Warriors

FACTFILE

Full Name: Kris Radlinski
Date of Birth: 9 April 1976
Birthplace: Wigan
Height: 6ft 1in
Weight: 14st 4lb
Club: Wigan Warriors
Position: Full-back or centre
Nickname: 'Rad' or 'Radders'
Caps: Great Britain 5, England 5, Academy 3
Medals: Premiership 1995, 1996; Regal Trophy 1996; Championship 1995, 1996
Tours: Papua New Guinea, Fiji and New Zealand 1996
Honours: Harry Sunderland Trophy 1995

Polish grandparents. My family came to England during the Second World War. I can't speak any Polish, but my Dad can manage a little.

On match days I arrive at the ground a good hour before the kick-off. I don't suffer from nerves, but I start to feel the tension about 20 minutes before kick-off. When the fixture is away from home, we generally arrive at the venue an hour-and-a-half early so we can stretch our legs with a walk.

2.30pm

When the afternoon is free, I go for a game of golf with Andy Farrell, Gary Connolly, Henry Paul, Nigel Wright and Craig Murdock. More often than not, we play on a local course but occasionally travel out to Liverpool or other destinations to make it more of an event. Golf is a great way to relax. We put £10 each into a prize fund – the winner taking all. I also help out at home if there is a job to be done. Last year I worked with my dad laying a new patio. Left on my own, I like to take a nap in the late afternoon.

8.00pm

If there is no game the following day, I socialise with the other players. They are a great bunch. We have formed a bachelor club and there is never a dull moment.

Whenever asked, we attend special functions at the club, such as 'Player of the Month' presentations by the sponsors. Coke is one of my favourite drinks. I am usually game for a laugh – and I'm especially fond of barbecues. But I always take things easy the night before a game. I'll be in bed fairly early after watching a video or a film on television.

Playing to Win How Super League coaches motivate their teams

Andy Gregory of Salford Reds

Salford Reds lively boss Andy Gregory loves to coach from the touchlines during matches in order to be as close to the action as possible. Many people wonder why he does not sit in the stands wearing headphones like other coaches. And messages have been sent from the Rugby League to that effect as well. But former Great Britain scrum half Andy says: "I want to be where I am most useful as a coach – and that is on the touchlines. I don't see why not. That's the way I enjoy it".

Andy Gregory

Gregory works on motivation every day of the week as he prepares his team for a game. It is not something he would ever leave until the last minute. He explains: "By the time the match comes around, I expect all my players to be fully focused. But I always talk to them about prime objectives shortly before kick off. I try to impress upon them that it is basically down to how much they want to be successful. The chairman usually comes into the dressing room as well to wish them luck. I'm always in the dressing room at half time talking about what we have done right and wrong. But I never blow my top if things are not working out. If we are losing, I tell them where we are slipping up and point out the absolute need to stick to the game plan we have worked on in training sessions. We talk constructively. If I need to criticise individuals, I will do that at some other time. And although I always look at statistics, I don't need these figures to tell me who is doing the work and who is not."

Shaun McRae of St. Helens

Success has brought special motivation problems for St. Helens boss Shaun McRae. He believes his team are most vulnerable when they are facing opposition everyone expects them to beat! And Saints have become so renowned in Super League that they are expected to come out on top against 95 per cent of the teams they meet. "The games to beware of most are those where fans and media predict an easy win," says Shaun. "Sometimes it rubs off on the players and we have got to be guarded against complacency. I tell the players that every match is worth two points, whether we are up against the team running last or the team at the top of the table.
"Self-motivation is the hardest thing of all. Even though we are in a team sport, it comes down to individuals at the end of the day. Success is a motivator in itself along with financial reward, but even if you took both of these factors away, the modern-day Rugby League player is such a fine athlete that he would still want to perform well because of his inherent qualities to compete.
"It is that competitive spirit which continues to drive them on week in and week out. At St. Helens, we always set long-term and short-term objectives."

John Pendlebury of Halifax Blue Sox

John Pendlebury, coach of Halifax Blue Sox, believes that Super League players are largely self motivated. "They know it is the only way to succeed," he says. "The most important part of my job is making sure that they prepare thoroughly and are ready for anything. If we get this right, everything else has a better chance of falling into place. I never go into the dressing-room until about 25 minutes before kick-off when I concentrate on certain individuals and points they need to be aware of. It is unusual if I stay longer than five minutes – but I often nip back in for another couple of minutes just before they take the field.

"My policy is to remain positive whether we are losing or winning. If things are going wrong, the team want answers and I am the man who is expected to give them. It's all about determination and sometimes this has to be reflected in the way a coach addresses his players for the message to sink in. I have a reputation for saying very little after the game because I have never regarded this as a good time for discussion on a performance."

Dean Bell of Leeds Rhinos

Fire and brimstone are preached by Leeds Rhinos coach Dean Bell – but only when the occasion demands it. "I try to assess the mood of the players and adjust the motivation accordingly," says Dean. "Different games can require different approaches. Sometimes, we are the underdogs and on other occasions we are favourites. I often remind the lads that they can fool the press, the coaches and the spectators but they can never fool themselves. They must be honest with themselves when it comes to assessing whether or not they have done their best."

Leeds begin their match day preparation by looking at positive video footage before going through a game plan as Bell highlights significant factors.

"After that, I leave the players alone until I speak to them again a few minutes before kick-off," says Dean. "At half-time I make a point of not entering the dressing-room too early because anything I say then might be lost on them before they go out. I give them a chance to rest and gather their thoughts before stressing the areas we need to work on. I say nothing at full-time since I prefer to leave my full assessment until I have watched the match video the following day."

Right: ***Shaun McRae***
Below: ***Dean Bell at the Rhinos' ground***

Reach for the SKY

Those brilliant Super League pictures you see on your TV set come to you via some amazing technology. How do they do that? You might wonder.

Space, the final frontier, has been conquered by the technology of Sky TV to bring live Super League action into homes across the world.

Pin-sharp pictures are beamed from outside broadcast vehicles to ground-based transmitters such as the BT Tower in London. From there they are sent 22,300 miles into space to be 'bounced' off the Astra communication satellite in orbit around the Earth. The Astra satellite returns the picture signals to Earth where they are picked up by satellite dishes – and that's when you see the pictures on your TV set.

Sky's Super League team, headed for the past six years by commentators Mike Stephenson and Eddie Hemmings, use up to 17 cameras at each game and travel up to 50,000 miles each year covering 75 matches. Their equipment includes super slow-motion cameras and seven replay video machines so that tries and incidents can be studied from several angles. The coverage includes on-screen graphics to inform viewers of statistics such as tackle counts, possession, 'hit-ups' and metres of ground gained.

The Astra satellite might be far away, but it brings those magic Super League moments to a TV near you

No one commands more respect in the team than the high cameramen, who spend much of their working life on a mechanical hoist 200 feet above the pitch. It goes without saying that they are not afraid of heights! Strong winds and lightning are the main concern as they work on their lofty perch. At the first hint of lightning, they don't wait for an invitation to descend to ground level as quickly as they can! Now, after many hard winters working in appalling weather conditions, no one appreciates the arrival of summer rugby more than they do.

Eddie and Stevo

The main stars of Sky's line-up are undoubtedly Mike Stephenson and Eddie Hemmings, whose wit and informed comment has identified them as leaders in their profession. Such is their impact that in the first Super League season, more than 5.5 million people watched live matches at home – an increase of 35 per cent on the previous year.

Mike Stephenson, better known as 'Stevo', is a former Great Britain star who scored a try in the World Cup victory in France in 1972. He led Dewsbury to their only championship success in the same season before signing for Australian club Penrith Panthers for a then record transfer fee of £20,000. After retiring from the game, Stevo worked for a variety of newspapers and radio stations in Sydney. He is now recognised as a major voice in the game.

Eddie Hemmings converted from soccer, having started his media career with local radio and newspapers on Merseyside in the 1970s when he followed Liverpool FC into Europe. His love affair with Rugby League began when he moved to BBC network radio in 1982. He met Stevo in 1988 when they became an instant hit working together on coverage of Great Britain's tour of Australia for radio.

Eddie and Stevo – Super League's double act. The sky's the limit for this dynamic duo

If it's on the pitch, it'll be seen on a screen inside the outside broadcast van – and in a split second it's on your TV set

Brothers in Arms

Brothers Robbie and Henry Paul were inseparable growing up in New Zealand. Now they are dazzling rivals in Super League. Robbie, aged 21, is skipper of Bradford Bulls. Henry, two years older, is a key player for Wigan Warriors. Here they talk about each other's qualities.

ROBBIE ON HENRY

Brothers don't come much closer than Henry and I. In fact, he's more than my big brother, he's also my best friend! When we were kids in New Zealand, I used to kick around in his shadow. And while we have never gone out to beat each other, there is a competitive spirit inside of us which is essential to our success.

Henry's best qualities are his magic feet and excellent balance. There is no one better at escaping from tight situations. Although he is close to being the complete player, he can be impatient and take risks. This can be his biggest downfall – but it is also what makes him special. It's wonderful when he attempts something out of the ordinary and it comes off. This is what the fans like.

In our younger days, I made more representative teams than Henry did. But when I arrived in England and saw how successful he was, I just wanted to be as good as him. He told me to have confidence in my own ability and to take on opponents.

Henry is a gentleman and a sensible person. I am not surprised he has made it to the top because he has been a cut above the rest all of his life. If there was anything he could not master, he would just keep doing it until he got it right. His eagerness to be Number One was the main thing I remember about him when we were kids. As well as excelling in sport, Henry had no trouble passing exams at school. He was in the top class while I was more of a free spirit at art school.

It's difficult to identify his best achievement because he has done so much already. He was junior Kiwi captain and played for Wigan at the age of 20. He has appeared at Wembley and represented his country at top level.

It would be great if we played in the same club side one day. It might cost some club a lot of money! But Henry is welcome to come to Bradford whenever he likes. That's my wish for the future! We played together as teenagers in New Zealand and we go well together.

FACTFILE

Full Name: Henry Rangi Paul (Rangi means 'sky' in Maori)

Date of Birth: 10 February 1974

Birthplace: Tokoroa, North Island, New Zealand

Height: 5ft 11 1/2in

Weight: 14st

Club: Wigan Warriors

Position: Utility back

Previous Club: Wakefield Trinity

Caps: New Zealand 6

Medals: Challenge Cup 1995; Premiership 1995, 1996; Regal Trophy 1995, 1996; Championship 1995, 1996

Honours: Junior Kiwis skipper 1993

HENRY ON ROBBIE

What I remember most about Robbie as a kid was his cheek. He was bright as a button and would never let anyone pull the wool over his eyes, let alone me. I don't recall falling out.

Although we look similar in some ways, Robbie's make-up is different. He was the smallest in his age group at school, but invariably one of the best. He was no Einstein when it came to exams, yet seemed able to cruise through them all without studying too much. As the elder brother, I was the one who had to win all the time. Robbie could not beat me at anything…until we grew older.

We have become closer as we have grown older. When I first came to England at the age of 19, Robbie was full of questions on what it was like over here. I was delighted when he got the chance to sign for Bradford Bulls. I knew he had the makings of a great player. I wanted him to play first grade as soon as possible, but I must admit that I am a little surprised how far he has come in so short a time. He has great vision and his electrifying pace off the mark makes him extremely dangerous. He can spot a gap where others can't.

If any improvement needs to be made, it is in his defence. But he is only young and getting stronger in this department all the time, as we saw last season. I am always asking Robbie about training techniques because it seems to me that they get up to some clever things at the Bulls.

Robbie gave the performance of his life in the 1996 Silk Cut Challenge Cup Final when he won the Lance Todd Trophy and became the first player to score a hat-trick of tries. It was the greatest individual display I have ever seen.

Maybe Robbie and I will play together in the same club side one day. If it ever happens, I would want to play stand-off with Robbie at scrum-half because I believe we could link together very well. Whenever we play against each other, I look on Robbie as just another opponent. I don't pay him special attention because I am too busy worrying about all the other players. However, I always make a point of reminding my team-mates at Wigan that he has a good side-step and should be treated with respect.

We are easy on each other, no matter who wins or loses. After all there is always going to be another game and a chance to even the score.

FACTFILE

Full Name: Robbie Rawiri Paul

Date of Birth: 3 February 1976

Birthplace: Tokoroa, North Island, New Zealand

Height: 5ft 9in

Weight: 12st 8lb

Club: Bradford Bulls

Position: Scrum half

Tours: Junior Kiwis to Australia 1994

Honours: Super League Player of the Year 1996; Lance Todd Trophy 1996

Henry** (left) **and Robbie** (far page) **get down to business
*Below: **The brothers clash***

Beat Stevo Quiz

20 questions from Sky TV commentator Mike Stephenson

1 When a red card is shown by a referee, it means that a player has been sent off. What does a yellow card indicate?

2 What is the biggest ever crowd for a Rugby League match?

a 97,550
b 112,600
c 102,569

3 Which Under-11s schoolboy side won the inaugural Wembley curtain raiser before the Challenge Cup Final in 1975?

4 Wigan won the Challenge Cup eight years on the trot from 1988. Who was the only player to appear in every game?

5 Which Australian club is known as The Sharks?

6 The Harry Sunderland Trophy is presented to the man of the match in which final?

7 Which club plays at Headingley?

8 What is a 'bomb'?

9 Who is nicknamed 'Rad' or 'Radders'?

10 Name the clubs the following stars play for:

a Paul Forber
b Karl Harrison
c Richie Blackmore

10a

4

10b

10c

11 Name the Australian coach who took St. Helens to a cup and League double in his first season in charge.

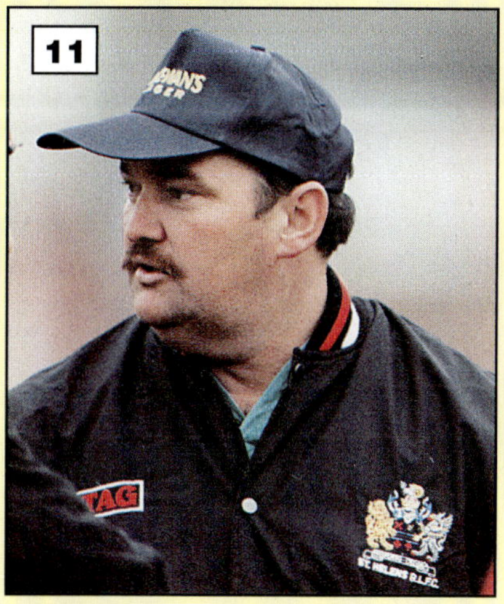
11

12 John Harrison and Barrie Jon Mather share the record for being the tallest to play at Wembley. How tall are they?
a 6ft 4 in.
b 6ft 7 in.
c 6ft 11 in.

13 Who is the youngest player to captain Great Britain?

13

14 Which of the Paul brothers scored most tries in the opening season of Super League – Henry or Robbie?

15 What is a 'power play'?

16 Which St. Helens forward is named after the successful moon landing of 1969?

17 If the 'Tigers' were playing the 'Blue Sox', which clubs would you be watching?

18 Who scored Super League's first ever try?

19 Which club does Nick Pinkney play for, and where did he sign from?

20 Which two clubs did Paul Newlove play for before he joined St. Helens?

20

TURN TO PAGE 61 TO CHECK YOUR ANSWERS

Rocketman!

Apollo Perelini, a Western Samoan named after the rocket that took the first men to the moon, is making great strides to conquer new horizons in Rugby League.

Born at the time of the moon landing, Perelini has been a tremendous success since quitting Rugby Union in New Zealand and joining St. Helens in the summer of 1994. But his life today as a top RL star and devout Christian is far removed from his wild teenage years when he drank and smoked too much and became involved in gang fights.

The youngest of eight children, Perelini admits that he was lucky not to end up in the hands of the police. And he dreads to think what might have happened to him if he had not found God. His outlook changed after a friend had introduced him to a Christian church. "I accepted God into my life and he now rules most of the things I do," he says. Perelini attends the Christian Life Church in St. Helens. He plays the drums in a church band and counsels North West youngsters with behavioural problems.

On the field, he is a powerful forward who can scatter opponents like ninepins. He has a phenomenal burst of speed which he first developed in Rugby Union as a flanker. He played in more than 50 provincial games while based at the North Harbour club and became a Junior All Black before switching national allegiance to Western Samoa, whom he represented on 16 occasions. In 1991, he helped

Blast off! Apollo takes some stopping as he powers into action

Western Samoa to beat Wales at Cardiff Arms Park and four years later returned to the Principality to represent his country in the Rugby League World Cup against France and Wales.

Perelini turned to Rugby League to follow Craig Innes, Matthew Ridge and his cousin Va'aiga Tuigamala after they had all played together at the Ponsonby club in New Zealand. Hearing that several British clubs were looking for forwards, Perelini contacted Manchester-based agent David McKnight and sent an action video of himself to St. Helens. Saints were impressed enough to invite him for trials – and just half a game in the reserves was enough to convince them to make an offer. Perelini's contract has since been updated to keep him at Knowsley Road until the year 2000.

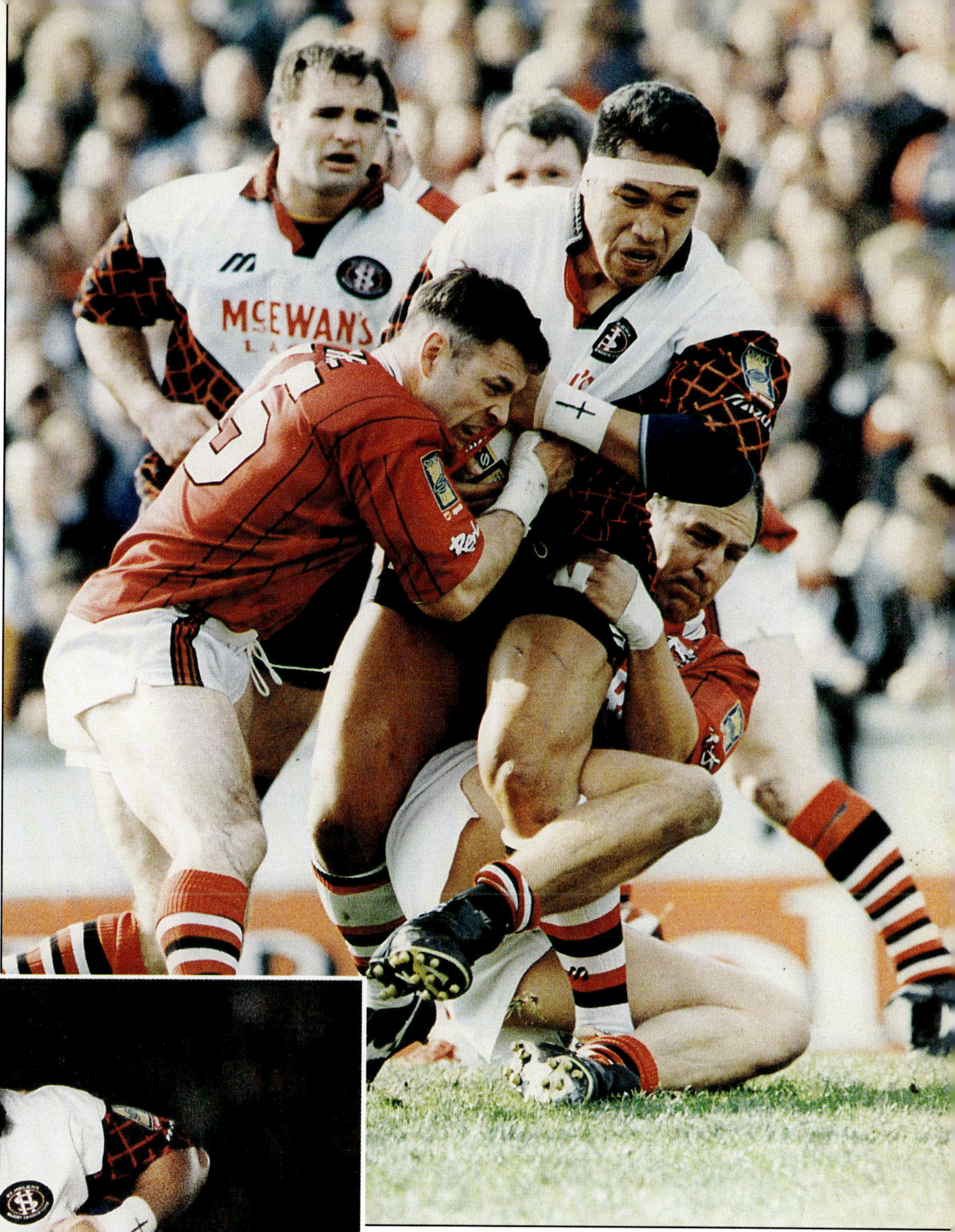

It's two against one – but Apollo can cope with the odds

FACTFILE

Full Name: Apollo Perelini
Date of Birth: 16 July 1969
Birthplace: Western Samoa
Height: 6ft
Weight: 16st 8lb
Club: St. Helens
Position: Prop forward
Nickname: 'Terminator'
Previous Clubs: North Harbour, Ponsonby, New Zealand
Caps: Western Samoa 2
Medals: Challenge Cup 1996; Stones Super League Championship 1996
Honours: Rugby League Writers' Player of the Year 1996

On the Circuit with Wigan fitness expert Chris Butler

Super League is making more demands on players then ever before. They have to be fitter and faster to meet the new challenges – and that means more hard work.

Weight-training

All players spend a lot of time on weight-training in the gym and many complete their own daily routines in addition to supervised sessions under the eye of their coach. Weight-training is perfect for increasing upper-body strength so essential in coping with the physical impact involved in Rugby League. It is also useful for helping players to increase their speed off the mark and sustain it over a distance. Even slow-coaches can be trained to run faster.

Being able to lift heavy weights once – as in competitive weight-lifting or body-building – is not what it is all about. The Wigan Warriors, for example, perform strength improving exercises which require them to lift heavy weights three to five times in succession. They also use pliometrics in circuit training which is designed to produce extra pace while tightening up joints and muscles to withstand bodily contact.

Lifting experience! Keeping fit means hard work on the weights

Other exercises

But there are lots of other standard exercises which help maintain fitness and health without the use of special equipment. The most common of these are sit-ups, jogging, sprinting, squat thrusts and press-ups.

Jogging is great for keeping fit. This is a basic part of training. Many players like to warm-up with a run around town. I often go with them. I recommend running for a minimum of 20 minutes for three or four consecutive days. Move no faster than a speed at which you can hold a conversation.

In sprint training, the Warriors hit 40 metres off a rolling start and 15 metres off a standing start. Leg speed and drive is what I look for. Squat thrusts are a demanding exercise. A normal rate would be one every other second for 60 seconds. Most of the Warriors can complete 80 in 60 seconds. With press-ups I ask the Warriors to do as many as they can in 20 seconds and then rest before twice repeating the exercise.

Building up a sweat! Good preparation in training is the key to doing well

Chris Butler is a former athletics coach who helped to develop David Grindley into an Olympic star. He joined Wigan five years ago and initially worked alongside 400-metre hurdler Bill Hartley.

Captain Fantastic

Focus on Wigan Warriors Skipper Andy Farrell

Some players are born leaders – and blockbuster Andy Farrell is one of them. He has captained teams at almost every level and became Great Britain's youngest skipper when he led the 1996 tour to Papua New Guinea, Fiji and New Zealand.

Farrell was two years younger than legendary Harold Wagstaff, who led the Lions on their 1914 and 1920 tours, and Brian Noble who was skipper on the 1984 trip Down Under. Just for good measure, Farrell was back in Australia two months later leading Britain's bid for the World Super League Nines trophy in Townsville. Indeed, Andy has achieved so much at the age of 22 that no one would be surprised if he sometimes pinches himself to make sure he is not dreaming.

Left: **Andy slips the ball out of a tackle**
Above: **A goal-kick heads for the target**

‘MAN OF STEEL’

FACTFILE

Full Name: Andrew Farrell

Date of Birth: 30 May 1975

Birthplace: Wigan

Height: 6ft 4in

Weight: 16st 2lb

Club: Wigan Warriors

Position: Loose forward

Nickname: ‘Faz’

Caps: Great Britain 10, England 5, Under-21s 1, Academy 5

Medals: Challenge Cup 1993, 1994, 1995; Premiership Final 1994, 1995, 1996; Championship 1994, 1995, 1996; World Club Challenge 1994

Tours: Papua New Guinea, Fiji and New Zealand 1996

Honours: Young Player of the Year 1994, 1995; Man of Steel 1996; Harry Sunderland Trophy 1996

Powerfully built and standing 6ft 4in tall, he is recognised as one of the most skilful and mobile backrow forwards in the world. At one stage he weighed around 18st 8lb but trimmed down to just over 16st to meet the demands of Summer rugby and the intensity of Super League. “The main thing is I am as strong as ever,” he says. “There would be no point losing weight if it meant losing power.”

Rugby League is a family affair for Andy now that he has been joined at Wigan Warriors by twin brothers Chris and Phil, who are five years younger. The trio are ambitious to make history by packing down together for the Warriors and going on to link up for Great Britain one day.

Responsibility comes naturally to Andy, who committed his future to Wigan when he was only fourteen, and made his debut in the first team only two years later. He skippered the Great Britain Academy side.

He has received a prestigious ‘Man of Steel’ award as well as the Harry Sunderland Trophy as man of the match in a Premiership Final. Among his winners medals he treasures nothing more than the three he picked up from Silk Cut Challenge Cup Finals at Wembley.

Yet when he was ten years old, Andy was more interested in Soccer than Rugby League. It was only on attending a Graeme West Summer School that he turned to the oval ball game. After joining Orrell St. James Juniors, he had an outstanding career in schools rugby before turning professional in 1992 with Wigan, when he was seventeen. The following year he became the youngest forward to represent Great Britain when he scored a try on his debut against New Zealand at Headingley. He also won Under 21 honours and took the ‘Young Player of the Year’ award after playing throughout the 1994 Ashes series against Australia.

Leader of the pack! Andy spells danger running with the ball or kicking for position

Pick of the Pics

There's nothing to compare with Super League for thrills, spills and non-stop action. These pictures tell their own story.

It's that man Perelini helping to up-end Platt of Salford Reds

Bradford's Danny Peacock crashes over for a try against Wigan Warriors

St. Helens stand-off Tommy Martyn is held by Castleford

The Bulls lock horns with the Saints at Wembley

Tulsen Tollett (London Broncos) beats Mick Cassidy (Wigan Warriors)

No way through for Wigan's Simon Haughton

French Connection

Pioneers PSG Rugby League have bravely carried the Super League flag in Europe since being born in a blaze of glory in Paris in the inaugural season of the competition.

After attracting an opening night crowd of 17,873 and losing only one of their first four matches, PSG narrowly avoided relegation when they finished next to the bottom. But there was stronger resolve for the second campaign following a total revamp and the capture of stars from Down Under.

A new management structure and limited company were also brought into place, in accordance with French law, to further stabilise the club and encourage the involvement of entrepreneurs on the board. The new company allows for up to two thirds of the shares to be taken by foreign investors, the French Rugby League taking one third.

With the success of PSG vital to ambitions in Europe, English help has come from Robert Elstone (General Manager), Harry Jepson (Chairman) and Rebecca Cove (Football Manager), but the club will be run by the French in the long-term.

More English expertise was introduced in May '97 when former Oldham Bears boss Andy Goodway was appointed to replace Peter Mulholland as coach. Hooker David O'Donnell, a former Manly Hooker, was given the job of starting as Skipper of

Right: ***David O'Donnell***
Below: ***Fabien Devecchi is tackled by St. Helens Paul Newlove***

Above: ***PSG's Charlety Stadium***
Right: ***Tony Priddle***

the squad, which prepared in Sydney over the winter. More experience was added in the shape of ex-St. George forward Tony Priddle, twice an Aussie Grand finalist and now in the process of rebuilding his career. Former North Sydney scrum half Jason Martin was also seen as a key figure along with the ever-present Jason Sands (top yardage man in 1996), Kiwi Phil Bergman and backs Deon Bird and Jamie Olejnik. French players who remained with the club for 1997 were Didier Cabestany (top tackler of 1996), Fabien Devecchi, Pierre Chamorin (the first French player to be offered a two-year contract) and Pascal Jampy. In an effort to boost the Gallic content of the side, French coach Michel Mazare and former French Test skipper Patric Entat were appointed to take charge of recruiting top French junior talent.

The PSG side are based at the magnificent Charlety Stadium to the south of Paris. PSG are the only cross-Channel side in Super League and, as such, the most travelled. In the course of a season they will cover more than 12,000 miles, mainly by jet.

The players live in a hotel in the Parisian village of Bougival and train at a sports ground on an island in the River Seine. For fixtures in England they travel the day before the game from Charles de Gaulle Airport to Manchester, and generally travel back the following day after staying in a top class hotel.

PSG gained their Super League first win on English soil in March when they travelled to the Don Valley Stadium and defeated Sheffield Eagles – the team they beat in the opening fixture in Paris last year.

Parisian support for the team is undiminished, and just as vociferous, despite the arrival of so many overseas players.

Signs and Signals

Referees' decisions explained

Referees indicate their decisions by holding up coloured cards or by signalling with their hands and arms. Here's what they all mean.

DISMISSAL

The referee holds up a red card to indicate he is sending off a player. Four main offences require this action – striking, high tackles, dropping knees first on an opponent and dangerous throw tackles. A dismissed player cannot return to the field. If guilt is determined at a subsequent meeting of the disciplinary committee, the player can be suspended for a number of matches. Players sent off on a regular basis will serve longer and longer sentences. Sometimes the committee will decide that sending off is sufficient punishment.

SIN BIN

The referee holds up a yellow card to indicate that he is sending a player to the sin bin. This action is taken for technical offences which are repeated or deliberately committed by way of 'spoiling tactics' in a try-scoring situation. Among the main culprits are players who commit 'professional' fouls by consistently lying on opponents to slow the game down so that defences can re-group.

ON REPORT

The referee will raise his arms above his head and cross his wrists to indicate that he is putting an incident on report for further study on video. This happens when the official cannot make a decision from the evidence available to him. Often, he takes the action when unsighted to an incident. He will also use the system, for example, in situations where a number of players have been involved in a fracas and the guilty need to be identified for disciplinary purposes.

BLOOD BIN

A touchline official holds up a green card with a white cross to indicate that a player is leaving the field for treatment to a wound. Initially, the card was red with a white cross, but this was discontinued to avoid confusion with the Red Cross health organisation. An additional substitution is allowed to those permitted if the injured player returns to the field of play within fifteen minutes.

STOPPING THE CLOCK

The referee will signal to the time-keepers to stop the clock when the ball cannot be played due to an injury, or special unforeseen circumstances. He indicates this by raising both his arms directly upwards with fingers extended. The clock is re-started when he waves an arm twice above his head with fingers extended. The match referee will stop the clock when he is consulting the video referee and will also call a halt if there is persistent time wasting.

AWARDING A TRY

The referee will point with an outstretched arm to confirm that a try has been scored. He will do this after checking the position of the touch-judges and will consult if necessary. A successful goal-kick is confirmed by the referee raising his arm in unison with two touch-judges who raise their flags.

KNOCK-ON, FORWARD PASS AND OFFSIDE

A knock-on is indicated when the referee gestures with his hands and arms that the ball has been pushed forward. He signals a forward pass by sweeping both of his arms forward in a passing motion and will indicate offside by sweeping one arm backwards in the direction of the offending team. He will stop play in each case by blowing his whistle and will generally order a scrum unless the offence has been committed on the sixth tackle, when the hand-over of possession is enforced.

Animal Crackers

Wacky mascots are all part of the fun of Super League. Some have become so popular with touchline antics that they are as well-known as the players

Sheffield started the trend by bringing in a fan to parade as a giant eagle around Don Valley Stadium.

Salford Reds have brought in Daredevil Duck, **Warrington** have the Wolfman and **Leeds** have Ronnie and Rita Rhino.

Castleford got in on the act by coming up with Tigerman while they split their sides laughing at **Oldham** over the antics of Buster the Bear, already a 'best mascot' award winner. **Bradford** also have a roaring success in Bullman – and there's twice the fun at Odsal Stadium now that he has been joined in a double act by his younger brother. **Halifax Blue Sox** also have an hilarious double act in Billy and Bluey.

It's a dog's life at **St. Helens** for the mystery fan who dresses up in a St. Bernard costume each week to help entertain the crowd – but he wouldn't have it any other way. Neither would supporters who look forward to him cavorting around the pitch in his larger than life Disneyland-style outfit before the match and at half time.

The cheeky St. Bernard loves nothing better than to chase a rival mascot up and down the

THE MASCOTS

touchline and to engage in mock battle with the crowd roaring him on. There's always a happy ending, of course, before the teams come out and engage in the real action.

The St. Helens mascot is so popular that he receives a mountain of fan mail each week from fans of all ages. He even has his own column in the club programme! Saints are keeping his identity secret – because they don't want to spoil the mystique. It's a little bit like when people dress up as Father Christmas. No one wants to know who they are because it's better to believe they are real!

Right: ***Saints fans join in the fun by painting their faces***
Left and below: ***The wacky line-up***

Focus on **Paul Sculthorpe**

Paul Sculthorpe became a full Great Britain international at just 19.

Q What do you remember about your first team debut?

A We beat Salford at home. I was made up because the first time I touched the ball, I made a long break and set up a try.

Q Who has been the biggest influence on your career?

A My parents and Ken 'Tug' Wilson, a former Oldham player, who used to train with me.

Q Who are your heroes?

A Ray Price, an Australian forward known as the 'Praying Mantis', and Ellery Hanley.

Paul finds the thick of the action in attack and defence for the Wolves

Q Who are the toughest opponents you have encountered?

A The New Zealand Test side.

Q What is your best memory of your first season at Warrington?

A Winning a first team place.

Q Do you have any superstitions?

A Clean boots! I won't turn out unless they are spick and span. And I don't walk under ladders at any time!

Q What do you like most about being a professional player?

A Keeping fit.

Q How would you describe yourself?

A Relaxed. Ambitious to succeed.

Q What music do you prefer?

A Anything from the pop charts.

Q What is your favourite food?

A Pasta, chicken and rice.

FACTFILE

Full Name: Paul Sculthorpe

Date of Birth: 22 September 1977

Birthplace: Burnley

Height: 6ft 3in

Weight: 15st 5lb

Club: Warrington Wolves

Position: Backrow forward

Nickname: 'Scully'

Caps: Great Britain 5, England 2, Academy 2

Tours: Papua New Guinea, Fiji and New Zealand 1996

Focus on **Steve Blakeley**

Steve Blakeley is one of Super League's top stars – and a driving force behind Salford Reds' bid for honours.

Q What do you remember about your time at Wigan?

A Skippering the Alliance side and scoring a try on my first team debut against Featherstone Rovers after going on as a substitute.

Q What led to your transfer to Salford?

A My opportunities were limited at Wigan because they had two world class stars at half back in Andy Gregory and Shaun Edwards. When Salford came in I jumped at the chance.

Q How long did you have to wait to make your debut at the Willows?

A I signed on the Wednesday and made my first appearance against my old club, Wigan, four days later.

Q Who has been your biggest influence?

A My father and Alan Hodkinson, who coached me as an amateur. When I went to Wigan, Graeme West was very good with me.

Q Who were your heroes when you were younger?

A Coming from Leigh, I thought John Woods was absolute magic. I was captivated more because he played stand-off, just like me.

Q Who are the toughest opponents you have come across?

A Wigan have been the toughest team to beat – but St. Helens are building up their reputation.

Q What was your first big achievement?

A Being selected for England and playing against Wales and France in the European Championship. I was also proud at being made skipper of Salford when we won the First Division Championship and clinched promotion to Super League.

Smart mover! Steve sidesteps away from St. Helens' forward Apollo Perelini

Q What has been your worst injury?

A I had problems on and off with my groin for two years. An operation didn't help much and I saw one specialist after another. Hopefully it's sorted out now.

Q What is your most treasured possession?

A My first England jersey takes pride of place. There is nothing to beat representing your country.

FACTFILE

Full Name: Steven Paul Blakeley

Date of Birth: 17th October 1972

Birthplace: Leigh

Height: 5ft 9in

Weight: 12st 7lb

Club: Salford Reds

Position: Stand-off

Previous Club: Wigan

Caps: England 2

Medals: Division One Championship 1996; Divisional Premiership 1995-96

Honours: Salford Young Player of the Year 1993-94

Q Are you superstitious?

A I avoid everything that is supposed to bring bad luck. I never walk under ladders. I also have a set routine when getting ready for a match. Jersey, shorts, socks and boots all go on in the same order every time.

The Name Game

Super League clubs have smartened up their act – on and off the field. They've not only adopted a dynamic new outlook, but trendy new nicknames as well.

***The spectacular image** of most premier outfits is now mirrored to that of gladiators or aggressive animals and birds of forest, field and jungle. And in all cases the identity change has come complete with a colourful new logo to help the marketing and sale of branded products.*

Wigan thought about becoming the 'Wizards' or the 'Warlords' before finally opting for the 'Warriors'. Compare that with the name they used to be known as – 'The Riversiders'.

There was also a big change in tradition at **Warrington**, who dropped their famous 'Wire' nickname to go on the prowl as the 'Wolves'.

Pioneering **Oldham** also jumped on the bandwagon by emerging as the 'Bears' after years under the banner of the 'Roughyeds'.

Bradford, previously known as 'Northern', considered becoming the 'Rams' before going instead for the appeal of alliteration and the 'Bulls'.

Leeds decided on a new name only after a poll among fans. The shortlist included 'Sharks', 'Bobcats', 'Lions' and 'Leopards'. Most supporters wanted the club to remain as the 'Loiners', but the vote went to the 'Rhinos' because of marketing influences.

Castleford, unable to become the 'Cougars' due to a clash with Keighley, opted instead to roar into action as the 'Tigers', a name suited to their traditional black and yellow colours.

Salford, new to Super League in 1997 under coach Andy Gregory, dropped the 'Red Devils' tag in favour of a subtle change to the 'Reds'.

Sheffield, a relatively new club, already had a

modern identity as the 'Eagles', while **St. Helens** had no reason to change from being the 'Saints'.

But **Halifax**, formerly the 'Thrum Hallers', broke the mould by blazing a different path to the rest and declaring themselves the 'Blue Sox'.

London were happy to remain as the 'Broncos', a title they only adopted in 1994–95.

Newly formed **Paris St. Germain** opted to be known simply as 'PSG Rugby League'.

Improve Your Game

Top advice from the stars of Super League

PASSING THE BALL
Steve McNamara (Bradford Bulls)

Passing demands vary depending on what position you play, but precision handling is especially crucial to half-backs and back row forwards like myself who set up play. The first step is to learn how to hold a ball correctly by cradling it in your hands. Fingers and thumbs are spread wide with palms facing inwards. Arms should be relaxed and slightly bent. Identify the player you want to pass to and focus on the target area – the receiver's lower chest and waist. Swing your arms to take the ball around to the side of the hips and pass in a straight line so that the ball arrives just in front of the receiver.

As the pass is completed, twist your upper body so that the shoulders are square to the ball receiver. Follow through with your arms and let your fingers and wrists direct the ball. Always be aware of the speed of the receiver. Remember, practice makes perfect. And don't forget to work on passing to the right as well as the left.

Above: ***Eagle on high Mark Aston.*** *Left:* ***Bradford's Steve McNamara***

PLACE-KICKING AT GOAL
Mark Aston (Sheffield Eagles)

My first golden rule is to place the ball correctly in an elevated position so that the point is clearly visible. It can be teed up on a mound of turf or sand or on a special plastic cradle. Most 'round the corner' kickers stand the ball upright. Aim the seam of the ball at the target when lining up the shot. Then stand directly over the ball with the non-kicking foot level with it and a small distance along side. The kicking foot is placed behind the ball.

Keep your head bent and focus on a spot one inch from the bottom of the ball. This will be the contact area. Step back from the ball a measured distance (this will vary according to personal choice) and make a final visual check on the target before commencing the approach.

Concentration is now vital. Take a few deep breaths if this helps. Everyone has a different routine to help them focus and shut out distractions. The approach run is made along a curved arc, the final two steps being straight. Always keep an eye on the ball and kick with the instep or side of the foot.

Aim to plant the non-kicking foot alongside the ball in exactly the same position as in the set-up so that the head can come forward over the ball at impact. Ensure that the kicking foot, after striking the ball at the bottom of the swing, follows through in a straight line for the posts. Stretch out your arms to aid balance.

Left: ***Roar of the Tiger from Lee Crooks***
Below: ***St. Helens' centre Paul Newlove.***

TACKLING TECHNIQUES
Lee Crooks (ex-Castleford Tigers)

Tackles come in four basic categories – head-on, side, rear and smother. The head-on tackle is the one which is required most often and the tackler has two options. He can passively use the ball carrier's momentum, or he can charge at him and forcefully knock him backwards. In each case the head of the tackler should be at the side of the attacker while the arms encircle the legs and grip tightly. With the power tackle, the legs drive forward so that the ball carrier is driven upwards and backwards.

When tackling from the side, target the thigh and make sure that you keep your head behind the ball carrier. Make contact with the shoulder and drive in hard. In the rear tackle, the defender should keep his head to the side of the ball carrier and the arms should encircle the thighs before sliding down to the legs. The smother tackle is performed to stop an attacker passing to a supporting player. Wrap your arms around his upper body to trap the ball. A team-mate can help you by going round the legs at the same time. Bring the opponent to the ground if possible. In all cases, the tackler should finish on top of the ball carrier.

SIDE-STEP AND DUMMY
Paul Newlove (St. Helens)

The side-step is a sudden change of direction aimed at catching the opposition on the wrong foot. Timing is of the utmost importance and experience counts for a lot at top level. The skill involves running at your opponent at maximum speed and committing him to a tackle. Then, when you are two to five yards away, drive either foot forcefully into the ground to change direction. Accelerate round him and straighten up.

Be prepared to side-step again if necessary. Try to develop your left foot action as well as the right so that you can move in either direction just as easily. To worry the opposition even more, work on building a good dummy pass into your repertoire. This is when the ball carrier motions to pass, but retains possession. The aim is to confuse the defence by causing attention to be diverted to a supporting player. The ploy works best when the defence are absolutely convinced that a pass is about to take place. So look at the receiver and swing your arms through as if you are parting with the ball – but don't let go!

Silk Cut Challenge Cup Final 1997

St. Helens 32   Bradford Bulls 22

Skipper Bobbie Goulding switched his kicking strategy from high level to low level to help St. Helens lift the Silk Cut Challenge Cup at Wembley for the second time running. After destroying the Bulls in the previous year's Final with towering 'bombs', crafty Goulding was equally effective with deadly grubber kicks which skimmed the ground like guided missiles. The surprise tactic worked twice in the first half to produce crucial tries for stand-off Tommy Martyn, who sprinted through on each occasion to pounce on the ball as it rolled over the line. Martyn also had a hand in two other tries and went on to win the Lance Todd Trophy by a landslide as Man of the Match. He polled 31 votes from Press judges to take the coveted award as convincingly as Bradford's Robbie Paul had done 12 months earlier.

But the Bulls, who last laid hands on the Cup in 1949, were left to wonder if the outcome might have been different had Aussie centre Danny Peacock enjoyed better luck. Peacock, scorer of Bradford's first try in the early stages, made it to the line again in the 32nd minute only to

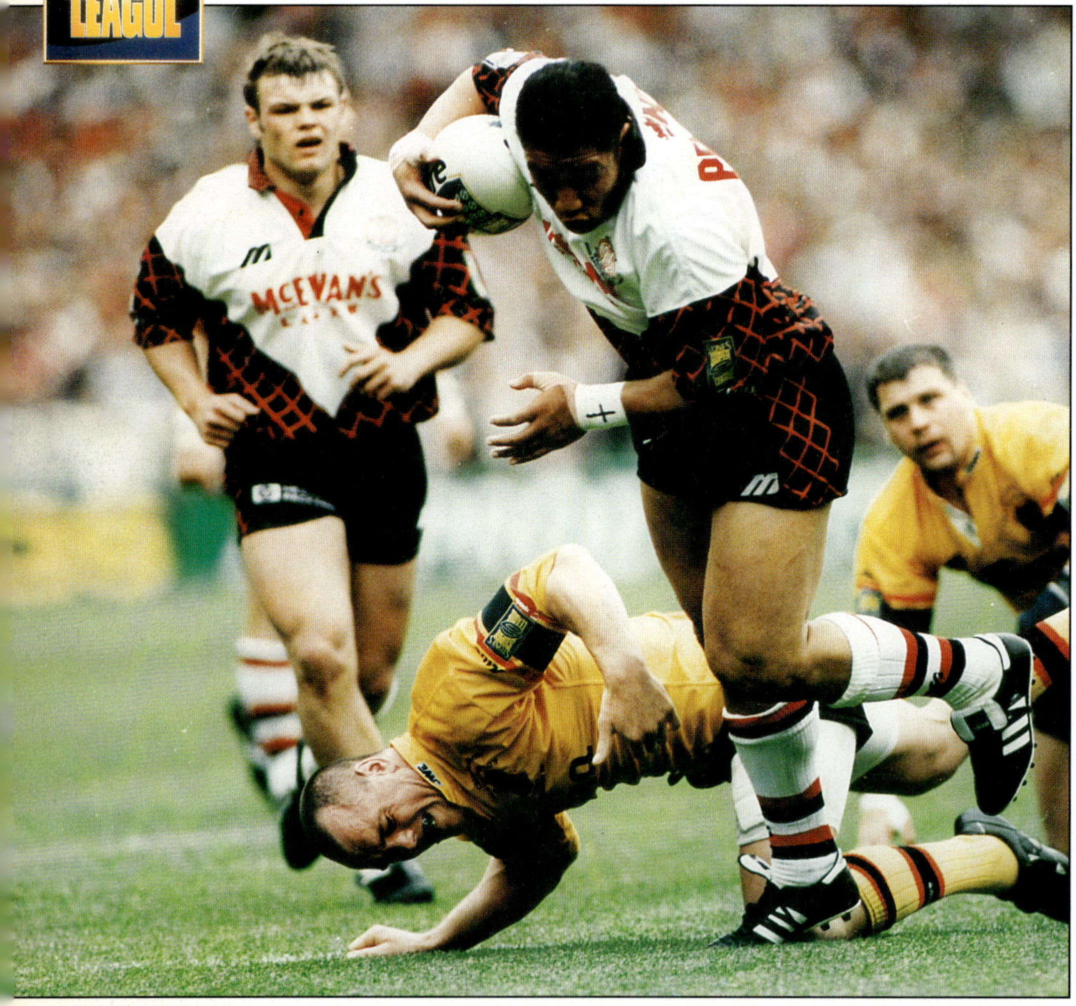

Left: ***Apollo Perelini on the rampage.***
Above: ***Bobby Goulding celebrates the victory when the hooter goes.***

have the ball knocked from his grasp by a tackle from Anthony Sullivan as he tried to touch down. This was an ironical twist of fate since a similar incident had cost St. Helens the Cup in 1987 when Mark Elia was deprived of a winning try when John Pendlebury's tackle caused him to lose possession over the line. It added to Bradford's agony when Peacock was denied again shortly after the interval when he was brought down by an ankle-

tap from Martyn with the try line open. From this escape, Saints set up a commanding 30–10 lead which was good enough to see them survive a spirited late rally by the Bulls.

It was the perfect result for impressive St. Helens, who were beaten by Batley in the first-ever Challenge Cup Final 100 years ago. But the defeat gave Bradford centre Paul Loughlin the record he had desperately hoped to avoid – a loser five times at Wembley! He is not going to give up trying. Paul, a former St. Helens star, believes he is young enough and fit enough at 30 to go on to Wembley again and chase that elusive winners' medal.

MATCH FACTS

St. Helens

Tries: Martyn 2, Hammond, Joynt, Sullivan

Goals: Goulding 6

Bradford Bulls

Tries: Peacock, Loughlin, Tomlinson, Lowes

Goals: McNamara 3

Half time: St. Helens 16, Bradford Bulls 10

Man of the Match: Tommy Martyn

Referee: Stuart Cummings (Widnes)

Attendance: 78,022 (capacity)

Left: ***Danny Peacock avoids the cartwheeling Steve Prescott.***
Below: ***Man of the Match Tommy Martyn lifts the Cup***

THE CHALLENGE CUP

The Challenge Cup was valued at just £60 when it was made in 1896. Today it is valued at £60,000. It was originally 36 inches high and weighed 189 ounces, but the ornate lid was reduced by several inches 30 years ago because it kept falling off!

The trophy – which still bears the title of the Northern Rugby Football Union Challenge Cup – was recently restored to its former glory by the removal of dents and scratches acquired over the years.

Batley, the inaugural winners of the Cup, received medals worth the grand sum of £3 3 shillings (£3.15) each, while runners-up St. Helens were presented with medals at £1 10 shillings (£1.50) each. Players in today's finals, in addition to receiving much-treasured medals worth around £500 each, can also look forward to winning bonuses of up to £5,000.

The 13,492 attendance at the first Final produced receipts of £614. Compare that with modern-day capacity crowds at Wembley of 78,000, taking more than £2 million.

Wigan have won the Cup a record 16 times, including eight consecutive victories between 1988 and 1995. Shaun Edwards made a record 10 appearances in Finals with Wigan, winning on all but one occasion.

Focus on **Tulsen Tollett**

Stand off Tulsen Tollett said goodbye to Sydney Harbour Bridge and waved hello to London Bridge when he came to England to play Super League in the capital.

He had packed his bags to seek fame and fortune with ambitious London Broncos…and to chase a dream of playing for Great Britain. That dream came true in his first season when he was selected for the Lions tour to Papua New Guinea, Fiji and New Zealand. Although he had grown up Down Under and represented Australia at under-19 level, he qualified for the Lions because he has English parents and was born in Hastings, East Sussex.

FACTFILE

Full Name: Tulsen Tollett
Date of Birth: 6 May 1973
Birthplace: Hastings
Height: 5ft 10in
Weight: 13st 7lb
Club: London Broncos
Position: Stand off
Nickname: 'Wallet'
Previous Clubs: Penrith Panthers, Parramatta
Tours: Papua New Guinea, Fiji and New Zealand 1996

Q Do you consider yourself British or Australian?

A Definitely British – even though I have an Aussie accent and I have my leg pulled about being a Pommie.

Q Did you always have ambitions to play for Great Britain?

A As a youngster, growing up in New South Wales, I wanted to play for the Kangaroos like most of my mates. But as I matured, my only thoughts were about pulling on a Great Britain jersey. It was what my parents wanted as well.

Q What is the origin of your name?

A My first name is Scandinavian and my surname has some French in it from my father's side of the family, going back a few generations.

Q Do you have any memories of England as a youngster?

A I was only seven years old when my family moved to Australia, but I never forgot Hastings. The first thing I did when I came back was to visit my Aunt and Uncle there and take a tour of the area.

Q At what age did you play your first game?

A I started with a local team when I was ten. I signed for Penrith Panthers when I was 17 and was in the first grade two years later. Then I made 40 first grade appearances with Parramatta.

Q What was it like playing for Parramatta alongside the famous Brett Kenny?

A It was a dream come true. Brett was my idol when I was a kid and I used to run around wearing a Parramatta No 6 jersey pretending I was him. After he had played his last game, he signed a photograph for me which I will keep for ever.

Q What was your reaction on being asked to join London Broncos?

A I knew it would be a good opportunity. I was friendly with a couple of players who were already here, which made the decision easier, and I jumped at the chance.

Q What was your first impression of England on arriving back?

A I landed in February, so the weather was bitterly cold. The wind blew right through me and for a moment I wondered "What am I doing?".

Q How do you rate the Broncos as a Super League force?

A We have knitted together well and we are looking forward to going on to bigger and better things. All the players are aware of flying the flag for Rugby League in the capital and the need for the club to succeed. If we play well as a team, everything else should follow.

Q Is there anything you miss about Australia?

A At first I longed for more sunshine, but now we are into summer rugby and there is no problem. I have lots of friends here. My main hobbies are water skiing and surfing. There's not much of that here unless I go to Cornwall. Then it's a matter of finding the time!

Q What are your ambitions?

A To continue my international career with Great Britain and help to make London Broncos one of the best teams in the world.

Tulsen shows the opposition a clean pair of heels as he sprints through a gap

When Worlds Collide

World Club Championship 1997

Super League went global for the first time with the launch last June of the World Club Championship – the biggest event in the game's 102-year history.

The World Club Championship, designed to find the best Rugby League side in the world, was contested by all 12 European Super League clubs and ten from Down Under, including New Zealand's Auckland Warriors.

Teams were split into four pools to play simultaneous matches in the Northern and Southern hemispheres. Matches were played in two phases, the first in June and the second in July to August. The top four teams from each hemisphere then played-off on a knock-out basis with the Final staged on October 18th.

Crushing defeats suffered by many European sides caused the RFL to appoint Joe Lydon to lead a commission to determine reasons why Australian sides are so dominant. Lydon, a former Wigan Warriors and Great Britain star, is studying all aspects of coaching, playing standards and player development.

Castleford Tigers' scrum-half Mike Ford is dumped by the Hunter Mariners' defence

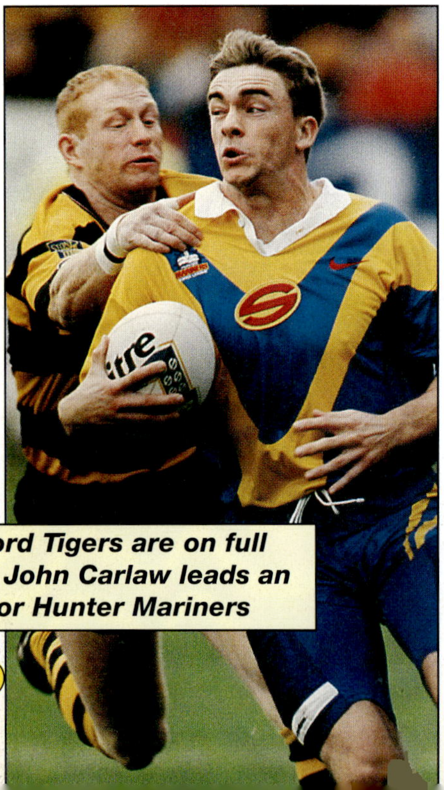

Castleford Tigers are on full alert as John Carlaw leads an attack for Hunter Mariners

Auckland full-back Matthew Ridge goes through the Saints' defence

Vila Matautia (St Helens) pushes off Sean Hoppe (Auckland Warriors)

Mike Forshaw (Bradford Bulls) is dumped by the Auckland defence

Bradford prop-forward Brian McDermott closes down Tawera Nikau of Cronulla Sharks

Brits Down Under

World Club Championship

Wigan Warriors' half-back Tony Smith finds a gap in the Canberra Raiders' defence

Crunch! Wigan Warriors' star Terry O'Connor feels the full force of a tackle by David Turner of Canberra Raiders

Got you! London Broncos flyer Martin Offiah is nailed by Canterbury's Daryl Halligan

Little v. large. Allan Langer (Brisbane Broncos) gets to grips with Andy Farrell (Wigan Warriors)

London Broncos' forward Peter Gill causes problems for Canterbury

Simon Haughton (Wigan Warriors) fends off Allan Langer (Brisbane Broncos)

Wigan's Kris Radlinski halts a Brisbane attack

Candid Camera

Yorkshiremen Andrew Varley and Simon Wilkinson are among Rugby League's most travelled photographers – and among the best at the job. It's their photos you can see in this book.

Andrew and Simon's special assignments have taken them around the world many times covering the sport they love for leading newspapers and magazines. Spectacular telephoto pictures are their trademark, but they are also experts at capturing bizarre or unusual scenes on camera.

Life is full of surprises – and Andrew and Simon are always ready to snap the moment regardless of whether they are in the jungle of Papua New Guinea, the Outback of Australia or on duty back home at Castleford's Wheldon Road. Here are just three favourite photos from their collection.

JUNGLE LOOK!

Opposite page: ***Spear tackle! Bobbie Goulding and Iestyn Harris go native while on tour to help local tribesmen show off the latest line in South Sea Island fashion!***

Above: ***How's this for tree-mendous support? Resourceful Rugby League fans in Papua New Guinea don't give up when they can't gain admission to grounds packed to capacity. They climb high into the foliage of the surrounding jungle – and watch from there!***

Right: ***Ripping yarns! Prolific Aussie try-scorer Scott Roskell gives everything for London Broncos – including the shirt and number off his back!***

Wing Wizards

Super League is blessed with many stylish and speedy wingers. But none create more excitement in flight for the line than keen rivals Jason Robinson and Tony Sullivan

Jason Robinson

Jason Robinson has become one of the most sought-after players in the world following a rapid climb to the top with mighty Wigan Warriors. Nicknamed 'Billy Whizz', he is an exciting attacker with an individual style and is known for bursting through defences in the most unlikely situations to score match-winning tries. He will dodge and dart, twist and turn and stop and start until the opposition are tied in knots. Once in the clear, his speed takes him to the line.

After starting his career at scrum half, Jason moved to the wing but often roams in field looking for work to help out his forwards. When it comes to hard yards gained from acting half back, he is consistently in the top five. In the Regal Trophy Final of 1996, he gained an incredible 235 yards from 17 drives in a performance any forward would be proud of.

Jason's speed off the mark makes him especially dangerous and he constantly works on this aspect of his game. At the snap of a finger, he is away like a rocket.

Two of his greatest tries were scored on his Great Britain debut against New Zealand at Wembley in 1993 – the season he was named Rugby League's Young Player of the Year. Fans are also unlikely to forget the two tries he scored at Wembley when Wigan last won the Challenge Cup against Leeds in 1995.

Spectacular tries are a trademark of Wigan's jack-in-the-box winger Jason

FACTFILE

Full Name: Jason Robinson

Date of Birth: 30 July 1974

Birthplace: Leeds

Height: 5ft 7½in

Weight: 12st 6lb

Club: Wigan Warriors

Position: Utility Back

Nickname: 'Billy Whiz'

Caps: Great Britain 4; England 7; Under-21s 1; Academy 2

Medals: Challenge Cup 1993, '95; Premiership 1994–96; Regal Trophy 1993,'95,'96; Championship 1994–96; World Club Challenge 1994

Honours: Rugby League Young Player of the Year 1993; Lance Todd Trophy 1995

Tony Sullivan

Class and style are embraced in equal measure by dashing Tony Sullivan, a winger who has been a model of consistency for Wales and St. Helens. His potential was revealed in his early days with Hull Kingston Rovers when he won Under-21 honours with Great Britain. But it was only after moving to St. Helens in 1991 that his career started to take off.

An experienced and mature player, Tony has a great positional sense and a fine turn of speed which has bought him many tries. For sustained running over a distance, few will match him other than team-mate Alan Hunte.

"It's all about having confidence in yourself," says Tony, who finished third top try scorer with 24 in Centenary Championship season, four behind joint leaders Martin Offiah (Wigan Warriors) and David Plange (Hull KR). He has been capped thirteen times for Wales. In fact, he did not miss a game for Wales for five years until injury ruled him out of the European Championship decider against England in 1996.

He made his Great Britain debut in 1991 against Papua New Guinea and toured with the Lions in 1996, playing in Tests against Papua New Guinea and Fiji and in two tests against New Zealand.

In addition to helping Wales win the European Championship in 1995, he figured prominently in the World Cup that year, scoring a hat-trick against France and another try against Western Samoa.

There's no stopping Tony Sullivan as he zooms away

FACTFILE

Full Name: Anthony Sullivan

Date of Birth: 23 November 1968

Birthplace: Hull

Height: 5ft 10in

Weight: 13st 7lb

Club: St. Helens

Previous Club: Hull Kingston Rovers

Position: Winger

Nickname: 'Sully'

Caps: Great Britain 5, Wales 13, GB Under-21s 1

Medals: Second division Championship 1990; Challenge Cup 1996; Stones Super League Championship 1996

Tours: Papua New Guinea 1990; Papua New Guinea, Fiji and New Zealand 1996

Academy Aces

The pro-am Academy League was formed in 1991 so that young players could enjoy the benefits of being associated with professional clubs.

One look at the teams in Super League provides evidence enough that the Academy is succeeding in its primary function of producing high quality Under-19s stars.

Of the 26 players who toured Australia with the Great Britain Academy squad in 1994, many are now household names in the top flight. Claims to fame have come from **Simon Haughton** (Wigan Warriors), **Mark Hilton** and **Jon Roper** (Warrington Wolves), **Paul Rowley** and **Simon Baldwin** (Halifax Blue Sox) and **Iestyn Harris, Francis Cummins, Ryan Sheridan and Graham Holroyd** (Leeds Rhinos). Among others hitting the high spots are **Jason Flowers** and **Nathan Sykes** (Castleford Tigers), **Sean Long** (St. Helens) and **Andy Craig** (Wigan), **Paul Cook** (Huddersfield) and **Lee Penny** (Warrington). Skipper **Paul Stevens**, then at Wigan, has since played with London Broncos and Rochdale. Other players have made it at First Division level.

Warrington could certainly not complain about the payback on their investment in Harris, who was sold to the Rhinos in a £350,000 deal in April '97. Sheffield Eagles have also done good business with Sheridan, whom they developed from raw state to finished product before

Halifax's brilliant young hooker Paul Rowley

Left: ***John Roper of Warrington Wolves***
Below: ***Wigan discovery Simon Haughton***

allowing his move to Leeds.

With one or two notable exceptions, the players who represented Great Britain Academy on the 1996 New Zealand tour are not quite as well known yet, but look certain to follow the same pattern.

Salford Reds wing or centre **Nathan McAvoy**, who was called from the Academy into the senior tour squad, has a great future ahead of him. Other exciting discoveries include **Paul Anderson** (St. Helens), **Jamie Field** (Leeds Rhinos), **Ian Watson** (Salford Reds), **Gary Broadbent** (Salford Reds) and **Daryl Cardiss** (Wigan Warriors).

Field, an agile prop forward or second row with great vision, was the tour squad's own choice as the outstanding player of the seven-match trip. Cardiss is rated a tremendous prospect for Wigan, even though it is never easy for a youngster to break into the first team at Central Park. 'Young players now have a focal point to aim for', says John Kear, Academy coaching director for five years before leaving for a leading role with Sheffield Eagles. 'Rugby League is regarded as an attractive career and it helps when players can be accommodated at a competitive level at an early age. We have provided a ladder to the top, the first rung being schools representative followed by the Academy, Alliance and senior first team rugby. Great strides have been made since a youth development policy was introduced five years ago. We are now comparable with the Kiwis, but still have some catching up to do on the Australians.'

Initially, the Academy was for players under 19 at midnight on August 31st of the new season. This has been changed to midnight on December 31st preceding the new season.

Making the Grade

By Iestyn Harris (Leeds Rhinos)

There are no short cuts to reaching the top in Super League. It takes a lot of hard work and dedication. Anyone giving less than 100 per cent effort will not make it. This is the golden rule which applies to all players at all levels, no matter what their age or natural ability.

Everyone has dreams. But it's one thing to be ambitious – and another thing to make those ambitions come true. To be the best, you have to beat the rest.

And this means staying at the peak of fitness, both mentally and physically. As standards improve in Super League, so does the demand on players.

While a match may only last for 80 minutes, there is lots of preparation and long hours of training to be undertaken in the week before hand. It is relatively easy to get in trim, but difficult to maintain the fitness level needed to compete week in, week out against the best teams in the country. The secret is to go out and enjoy it – just like I do. I revel in the training and I can't wait for match day. It gives me a real buzz.

My advice is to start young and listen to everything your coaches tell you. I was playing Rugby League at the age of nine. My grandad played professionally and my dad played for over 20

FACTFILE

Full Name: Iestyn Rhys Harris

Date of Birth: 25 June 1976

Birthplace: Oldham

Height: 5ft 10in

Weight: 13st 9lb

Club: Leeds Rhinos

Previous Club: Warrington Wolves

Position: Utility back

Nickname: 'Rolf' or 'Harry'

Caps: Great Britain 5, Wales 8, GB Under-21s 2, GB Academy 5

Tours: GB Academy to Australia 1994; Wales to America 1996; Great Britain to Papua New Guinea, Fiji and New Zealand 1996

Honours: International Player of the Year 1995

Balanced running is a feature of Iestyn's play

years as an amateur, so I guess rugby has always been in my blood.

I have always tried my best to play it well. And I can't imagine having a better job, even though it occupies me seven days a week. Apart from the training with the Rhinos, I put a lot of extra work in during my own time. There is nothing to compare with feeling fit. Reactions become quicker and you feel as if you can move mountains. Weight training is part of my schedule, but I don't go over board on it because it is not needed as much for the roles I play. I work more on ball skills and improving my pace and agility.

Speed off the mark is vital in the back positions, especially now that the game is quicker following the move to summer rugby. Players have to be ready for anything. Diet is also important. My typical breakfast is four Weetabix in a bowl of milk. I also eat a lot of fruit at all times of the day and evening. For main meals I enjoy chicken or turkey, vegetables and any kind of pasta. But I never touch junk food. I am not a big eater compared with some forwards. And I never eat anything at all before a match, no matter if the kick-off is in the morning or the evening. Alcohol is all right in moderation and I go out for a social drink once a week.

Competition for places is keen at Leeds, which is to be expected. So there is all the more reason for me to continue to look for ways to improve. I am only 21 and I have lots to prove yet. I was relieved more than anything else, when my future was sorted out and I was moved to Headingley from Warrington on a five-year contract last April. I had been listed at a £1.35 million but the fee which eventually changed hands was more in the region of £300,000, a record for the Rhinos. It was the chance I had been looking for to re-launch my career. My signing was likened to the day 45 years ago when Leeds signed the great Lewis Jones, who was equally at home, like me, playing stand-off or full back. I hope I can serve the Rhinos as well as Lewis in the seasons ahead.

Talented Iestyn stays cool under pressure for Wales

???? Teaser Time Test your knowledge and your memory

True or False?

1 Yorkshire's Geoff Clarkson is the game's most travelled player after being involved in a record 12 transfers.

2 Wigan were the first winners of the Rugby League Challenge Cup.

3 Mike Stephenson, the Sky TV commentator, is a former Great Britain player who scored a try to help win the World Cup Final of 1972.

4 The longest successful goalkick has been measured at 75 yards.

5 Martin Offiah was the first to score a hat-trick of tries in a Wembley final.

6 In 1998, sponsors Stones will complete a three-season deal which has been worth £1.7 million to the Rugby League.

7 Robbie Paul teaches in the Bradford classroom three mornings a week and tells young people about healthy living and staying away from drugs.

8 Wigan utility back Kris Radlinski collects baseball bats as a hobby.

9 One of Shaun Edwards' remaining ambitions is to complete a book on his life.

10 Each Super League club receives a basic payment of £850,000 per year from backers News Corporation.

Was Martin Offiah really the first to score a hat-trick of tries in a Wembley final?

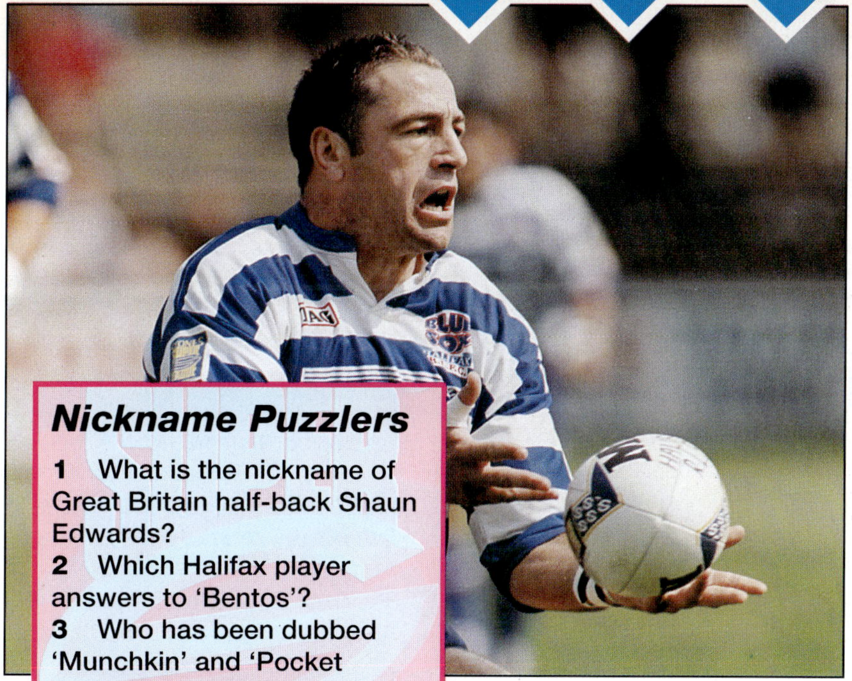

Nickname Puzzlers

1 What is the nickname of Great Britain half-back Shaun Edwards?
2 Which Halifax player answers to 'Bentos'?
3 Who has been dubbed 'Munchkin' and 'Pocket Battleship' at St. Helens?
4 He is known as 'The Penguin' at Bradford. Who is he?
5 What is the nickname of Great Britain star Tony Smith?

Above: ***Is this player nicknamed 'Bentos'?*** *Right:* ***Could this be 'The Penguin'***

Unscramble the letters to name these players

1 Yrag Ollyconn (Wigan Warriors)
2 Norkei Hamingcunn (St. Helens)
3 Onnsy Elnick (Bradford Bulls)
4 Tinmar Toncromp (Oldham Bears)
5 Ierich Moreblack (Leeds Rhinos)
6 Luap Melhu (Warrington Wolves)
7 Noed Dirb (Paris St. Germain)
8 Tinmar Sonpear (Halifax Blue Sox)
9 Ele Koorcs (Castleford Tigers)
10 Kcin Neypink (Sheffield Eagles)

Above: ***The ground of St. Helens.*** *Right:* ***The ground of Salford Reds***

Name the Super League grounds from these cryptic clues

1 Weeping Trees
2 Just Not Cricket
3 Bend From the Waist
4 Congratulatory Street
5 Safari Route

TURN TO PAGE 61 TO CHECK YOUR ANSWERS

Stars of the Future

Phil Larder, ex-Great Britain coach and a former RFL Director of Coaching, picks three stars of the future.

1 ADRIAN MORLEY (LEEDS RHINOS)

Adrian is one of the most outstanding second row forwards in Super League – a fact which was acknowledged when he was named in the prestigious Rothmans Coaches Select XIII for 1996. He was chosen for the side (at the age of 19) along with Warrington's Paul Sculthorpe, making them the youngest second row pairing to win this particular honour.

Adrian has made a terrific impact since signing for Leeds Rhinos from Eccles amateurs in 1994. Of all the players coming through, he has the most potential to go all the way over the next few years. He won two caps with Great Britain Academy against France in 1996 and toured Papua New Guinea, Fiji and New Zealand with the Lions later the same year.

An awesome runner and fine athlete, he had the misfortune to be sin-binned five minutes after going on as substitute for his Great Britain debut in the First Test against the Kiwis. Adrian was a try-scoring substitute in the Third Test and was also selected for the World Nines trip to Townsville, Australia, early in 1997.

2 KEITH SENIOR (SHEFFIELD EAGLES)

Keith has come on in leaps and bounds as an attacking centre since graduating with the Eagles from the club's Academy side in September 1994. He is the

Left: ***Adrian Morley has the potential to go all the way***

Right: **Keith Senior is Sheffield's quickest**
Below: **Nathan McAvoy will grab tries galore**

quickest player at Sheffield. An impressively direct and aggressive runner, Keith can break a defensive line and give excellent service to his wingman.

Keith's hard work was rewarded when he was selected for the Lions tour to Papua New Guinea, Fiji and New Zealand in the Autumn of 1996.

He made his Great Britain debut in a 72–4 victory in the first ever Test against Fiji, scoring a try in the 75th minute after going on as substitute.He also made an appearance as substitute when he replaced Stuart Spruce in the 55th minute of the First Test against New Zealand.

Facts

Born: 24/4/76
6ft 3in 14st 3lb

3 NATHAN McAVOY (SALFORD REDS)

Nathan caught the eye when the Reds were in the First Division. He stood out above the rest even though he was then aged only eighteen.

He is powerfully built and is extremely quick – just perfect for scoring lots of tries. He grabbed 20 in the Reds' championship season of 1996 and was one of the main reasons why they secured promotion to Super League.

Nathan is talented in a number of ways, but it is his exciting gift for finding gaps and making it to the try line which will make him a player to look out for in the years ahead.

He came briefly under my charge when he made his debut for England against Wales in the European Championship of 1996 and acquitted himself well. Consequently, I had no qualms about drafting him in from the Academy later that year to play for Great Britain in a mid-week tour game in New Zealand.

Facts

Born: 3/12/76
6ft 4in 15st 12lb

Competition

How much do you really know about Super League? Test your knowledge by answering these three questions – you could be a lucky winner in this great competition!

Top prize

We have two pairs of tickets to the 1998 Silk Cut Challenge Cup Final to be played at Wembley in May. We'll even pay your rail fare to get you there!

Runners-up prizes

Three runners-up will receive replica club shirts of their choice.

*A further ten runners-up will receive **'Battle for the Super League '97'** videos from Twentieth Century Fox*

Here's what you have to do:

Answer the following three questions – you'll be surprised how easy they are!

1 Who is this spaceman who would like to play rugby on the moon?

SUPER LEAGUE

2 How many clubs are in the Super League?

3 **Which club won the 1997 Silk Cut Challenge Cup?**

- Complete the entry form and send it to the address shown before 1 February 1998
- Send a photocopy if you don't want to cut the page
- The first two correct entries drawn on 1 February 1998 will each win a pair of tickets for the 1998 Silk Cut Challenge Cup Final. The next three correct entries will win replica club shirts of their choice. The next ten correct entries will win videos.

Super League Competition

Write your answers in the spaces provided

Super League 1

The player is: ______________________________

Super League 2

The number of clubs in the Super League is: ______________________________

Super League 3

The winners of the 1997 Silk Cut Challenge Cup were: ______________________________

Your Name: ______________________________

Age: __________ Chest Size (for shirt) **S** ☐ **M** ☐ **L** ☐

The club shirt I would like is: ______________________________

Address: ______________________________

____

____

______________________________ Post code ______________________________

Don't forget! The closing date is 1st February 1998

All entries should be sent to:

Super League Competition
Marketing Department
World International Ltd.
Deanway Technology Centre
Wilmslow Road
Handforth
Cheshire SK9 3FB

P L A Y T O W I N !

Did you Know?

Highest score

Huddersfield Giants hold the record for the highest score after beating Blackpool Gladiators 142–4 in a Regal Trophy game in November 1994.

Trophy winner

George Nicholls, the former Widnes and St. Helens forward, has the distinction of having won three of the game's most prestigious awards – Man of Steel (1978), the Lance Todd Trophy (1978) and the Harry Sunderland Trophy (1976).

Semi-final kings

Oldham Bears have had no luck in their quest to appear in a Challenge Cup Final at Wembley. They have reached the semi-final seven times – and lost them all.

Getting ahead

John Harrison once caused controversy at St. Helens by deliberately heading the ball forward to set up a try. It was a move rehearsed in training.

Fishy tale

It's the custom of Hull Sharks to present visiting officials with a box of locally-landed fish!

Royal rugby

Prop forward Aaron Pallalei, who played for Mansfield and Keighley, was a crown prince in the Royal family of Western Samoa!

Below left: ***Heads you win! John Harrison, a forward thinker at St. Helens***
Below: **George Nicholls**

Great escapes

Wigan had many close calls in winning the Challenge Cup for a record eight times on the trot. But their greatest escape of all came at Hull in 1994 when they recovered from 21–2 down to win 21–22. The drama and excitement continued into the dying seconds with Hull winger Paul Eastwood missing a comparatively easy penalty goal.

Oldham also looked doomed to defeat when they trailed 29–8 in the Second Division Premiership Final against Hull KR at Old Trafford in 1990. Then, in an amazing reversal of fortunes, Oldham tore the Yorkshire side apart with a five-try volley which swept them to victory 29–30.

Answers

Page 16/17 – BEAT STEVO QUIZ

1 Sin Bin **2 c** **3** Widnes **4** Shaun Edwards **5** Cronulla **6** Premiership Final **7** Leeds Rhinos **8** A tactical high kick **9** Kris Radlinski (Wigan Warriors) **10 a** Salford Reds **b** Halifax Blue Sox **c** Leeds Rhinos **11** Shaun McRae **12 b** (6ft 7 in) **13** Andy Farrell (Wigan) **14** Robbie (23 tries) beat Henry (22 tries) **15** Running the ball on the 6th tackle **16** Apollo Perelini **17** Castleford and Halifax **18** Frederic Banquet (PSG) **19** Sheffield Eagles (signed from Keighley Cougars) **20** Featherstone Rovers and Bradford Bulls

Page 54/55 – TEASER TIME

True or False?

1 True **2** False (Batley were the first winners) **3** True **4** True (kick by Castleford's Arthur Atkinson against St. Helens in 1929) **5** False (Robbie Paul for Bradford Bulls v St. Helens in 1996) **6** True **7** True **8** False (Radlinski collects baseball caps) **9** True **10** True

Nickname Puzzlers

1 'Giz' **2** John Bentley **3** Joey Hayes **4** Graeme Bradley **5** 'Casper'

Cryptic Corner

1 The Willows (Salford Reds) **2** Boundary Park (Oldham Bears) **3** The Stoop (London Broncos) **4** Wheldon Road (Castleford Tigers) **5** Knowsley Road (St. Helens)

Names Puzzle

1 Gary Connolly **2** Keiron Cunningham **3** Sonny Nickle **4** Martin Crompton **5** Richie Blackmore **6** Paul Hulme **7** Deon Bird **8** Martin Pearson **9** Lee Crooks **10** Nick Pinkney

Left: **Wigan's Jason Robinson** *Below:* **Terry Newton of Leeds** *Right:* **Steve McNamara of Bradford Bulls**

BLUE SOX
HALIFAX
R.L.F.C.
LEEDS RHINOS
ST.HELENS
RUGBY LEAGUE CLUB
WIGAN
FOUNDED 1872
RUGBY LEAGUE
CASTLEFORD RLFC